Alzheimer's: A Minister's Guide

In a world of darkness,
be someone's Northern Lights:
Fire Dance of Wonder!

Dwayne Cole

Parson's Porch Books

Alzheimer's: A Minister's Guide
ISBN: Softcover 978-1-936912-54-4
Copyright © 2024 by Dwayne Cole

All rights reserved. No part of this book may be reproduced or transmitted in any form or by any means, electronic or mechanical, including photocopying, recording, or by any information storage and retrieval system, without permission in writing from the publisher.

Parson's Porch Books is an imprint of Parson's Porch & Company (PP&C) in Cleveland, Tennessee. PP&C is a self-funded charity which earns money by publishing books of noted authors, representing all genres. Its face and voice is **David Russell Tullock** who you can contact at: dtullock@parsonsporch.com.

Parson's Porch & Company *turns books into bread & milk* by sharing its profits with the poor.

www.parsonsporch.com

Alzheimer's: A Minister's Guide

Preface

I pray that Jesus will be kind and merciful to us; and give us love and peace.
—Author's paraphrase of 2 John:1:3.

Follow the example of people who do kind deeds.
—3 John 1:11

Alzheimer's

Expressed in a haiku and a sonnet, this is my personal pain—

I touch the pain
of Alzheimer's each day
It doesn't go away

Life After Alzheimer's

Alzheimer's, a thief I did not invite!
Came through locked doors to steal
memory after memory from my wife.
Now she does not remember what is real.

I remember the joys of former days.
Dancing in sunshine, dancing in rain.
Must I learn to love in new ways?
Take her hand and dance with pain.

Memories of blue bird skies dripping—
Dripping down my cheeks and chin.
Will life ever be whole and sane again?

Must I learn to dance in new rhythm?
Hold pain close to beating heart.
Alzheimer's, a thief I did not invite!

As a minister, for 50+ years, I ministered to church members and families who were suffering from Alzheimer's. Now I am ministering at home personally, as I care for my wife.

Beth, my wife for 59 years, is suffering from Alzheimer's. She had the highest GPA in her college graduating class and won a full scholarship to seminary, where we met in a Greek class in 1965.

Alzheimer's is a life changing illness.
Now I am personally applying some of the lessons I taught church families who were dealing with Alzheimer's.

While I am a trained therapist, I am not a medical doctor. If you, or a family member seem to be suffering from Alzheimer's, you should go to your family doctor for an exam.

Introduction

Don't tell me that Alzheimer's is God's will.
That a powerful God controls everything.
An all-knowing and omnipotent God Is a
biblical myth beyond my belief.
Give me a relational God who lures us, toward
beauty, goodness, and wonder. A God in the
world and for the world.
Luring us to become our very best self. A God
who suffers our pain with us, saving all that
can be saved eternally. A God present in all
Gentle Teachings,
showing a love beyond race and gender. A
God clothed not as a powerful king, but as a
lowly humble servant.

The plane gains speed
Taking me to a place I did not choose
Where will it end

Frequently asked questions about Alzheimer's

(These are some of the questions I asked our family doctor daughter. You may have others. I have not given answers here. Research is ongoing and new questions and answers evolve. Take the questions you have to your primary care physician for up-to-date answers.)

1. How do doctors diagnose Alzheimer's and dementia?

2. Are an MRI and a cognitive memory exam the starting point in a diagnosis.

3. Are Alzheimer's and dementia the same thing? Is there a cure for them?

4. Why is weight loss associated with Alzheimer's?

5. How can I get the patient to eat and drink more?

6. Why is short term memory affected, but not long term? Are they performed in different parts of the brain?

7. Do all Alzheimer's patients revert to childhood?

Believing the Impossible

Some mornings I wake with seemingly impossible ideas bouncing up and down the corridors of my soul. I eat a hearty breakfast and start pondering adventurous ideas. I dress them with one of my favorite scripture verses:

Jesus' tender teachings gives us strength to face all things.
—Philippians 4:13

In these words my soul is prepared and moves toward tenderness with the challenge—

Kindness is at the core of being,
a focused awareness that begins in our soul
moves to our mind and heart.
Opening our eyes to see others as precious,
our ears to hear with compassion,
our hands to give comfort to others.

This book, *A Relational Hermeneutic of Kindness,* is at the heart of all my ministry and writing. It gives us a hermeneutic, a biblical lens through which we understand God, the Bible, and the world, and all people. You will find it helpful as you minister to those who are losing their grip on reality. It assures us that God is in the world, and for the world, in us and for us, luring us all toward truth, beauty, goodness, kindness, love, joy, and peace.

I use the term, relational, in this book, *Alzheimer's: A Minister's Guide,* as an hermeneutic, an interpretative lens for sharing communication tips for ministers and all care givers who deal with Alzheimer's patients.

GOD AS RELATIONAL KINDNESS

God as relational kindness, is the lens through which this book is written. A key biblical verse is—*"God, you brought me safely through birth, and you protected me as a baby at my mother's breast. From the day I was born I have been in your tender care, and from my birth you have been by my side."* (Author's paraphrase of Psalm 22:9-10).

When centered in God's creative loving kindness, we live and move and have our being in a circle of kindness that takes in the whole world. God is in all entities and for all, in the world and for the world.

Jesus was responsive to God's love aims and purposes for his life, and he became more God conscious with each self-actualization. Jesus' God consciousness, the very real existence of God in Jesus, enabled him to be more conscious of the needs of others in an ever-widening circle of loving kindness, and thus more fully divine and human.

Jesus spoke to God as a child would speak to a parent, confidently and securely. Jesus saw God like a kind father and nurturing mother.

The biblical image of faith in the time of Jesus was of a child wrapped in the folds of a mother's garment where there is security, comfort, nurturing, love, kindness, and hope.

God's loving kindness involves God as present in the world. True kindness feels what the other person is feeling, rejoicing in their joys and hurting with their pains. We would doubt that a husband loves his wife if he were not aware of her feelings as she deals with Alzheimer's; and if his feelings did not reflect her feelings and respond with kindness. As we experience God revealed in Jesus, we find God rejoicing with us in our times of joy and weeping with us in our times of sorrow. Our kindness toward others is based on this responsive kindness we see in God. My faith reflects the awe and wonder of God being in the world, in us, and for us, holding us close as a mother wraps her child in the folds of her garments or tenderly holds her child in her lap.

The God we meet in the beauty of nature is in us and for us, revealing goodness, grace, beauty, and kindness. God is tenderly present in all things.

The call of God toward kindness seen in Jesus' tender teachings is a call to all people. (See my book, *Gentle Galilean Glories: The Tender Teachings of Jesus*). For Christians, Jesus is the supreme example of loving kindness. To affirm this does not lessen the role of Moses for Judaism, Mohammed for Islam or Buddha for Buddhism, and other important religious teachers. Buddha said often, "My religion is kindness."

When any one relates to the God of creative possibilities, creative transformation occurs, bringing harmony and peace.

God's loving kindness is persuasive and luring, not coercive and demanding. Relational kindness does not seek to control with coercion. Relational power is greatest in its ability to influence others. If we love someone we do not seek to control or pressure them with promises and threats. Instead we try to persuade them with tender luring love to actualize the possibilities for goodness, beauty, and kindness. The gentle Galilean glories of Jesus define power in terms of loving kindness.

God as relational kindness is a vision that can change our world into one community knitted together by kind words and gentle loving actions. For a more complete development of a relational hermeneutic of kindness see my book, *A Relational Hermeneutic of Kindness*. This hope filled vision taps into the healing energy of kindness found in most religions and makes it the prism through which we understand God, the world, and all things. Kindness is the language known around the world.

Rainbows of Hope

Photos and Poems by
Dwayne Cole

**Relational tips for Alzheimer's Caregivers
Who Want to Be a Rainbow in Someone's Storm**

Relational Acronym

For me, the word, relational, is the key for opening doors to giving care to those suffering from Alzheimer's. All of life is relational from birth to death.

I prepared this acronym, **R. E. L. A, T. I. O. N. A. L.** as a way for understanding how to best minister to those suffering from Alzheimer's.

R. Reassurance. In relational kindness, **reassure** your loved one that God is with them, and you are with them in their pain and fear. They are afraid of losing everything that is precious to them.

While serving as a pastor, I would say to the spouse and church family, "As this loved one loses their short term memory, we will become their memory, remembering for them." If in a conversation they say the wrong name of a grandchild, do not correct them. Smile, and say, "We have wonderful grandchildren. You have always showed great love for them."

E. Empathy. In relational kindness, empathy is an umbrella term, gathering healing love energies that flow from one person to the other, singing to heart and soul. Do not remind them of what they cannot do. Gently show them what they can still do. Relational love allows you to put yourself in their position and feel what they feel and fear. When the whole Church family practices this empathy it becomes a powerful garden of energy where flowers blossom and butterflies flit from rose to rose.

The heartbeat of my nature poetry is empathy, uniting science and the humanities in a clear voice that brings healing to broken lives. My wife, Beth, who is now suffering from a mild form of Alzheimer's, mild in the sense that it is not marked by dementia, was a professional editor and manager of editor's.

She edited many of my poetry books. Now she will pick up one of my 32 books, and say, "I don't believe I have read this one." Even though I knew that she had edited the book, I do not correct her. I say, let me read some of the book for you. I take, *Snowshoe Hare Beauty,*

SNOWSHOE HARE BEAUTY

Photos and Poems
By

Dwayne Cole

and read from pages 35 and 38—

    All nature's seasons
bring to us the sweetest gifts
    Flower blossom kisses

      I bring a flower
The sweetest I could find
   Come and dance with me

L, Listen. Listening is an art form that has to be cultivated. Most conversation breaks down when we stop listening. It is especially hard to take a deep breath and listen when your wife with Alzheimer's asks for the tenth time in a day, "When did you start writing poetry?" Instead of saying, "You have asked me that nine times today already." When Beth ask me that question, I take a deep breath, and say, "Since I first looked across the Greek class at the seminary and saw your beautiful warm smile."

At that moment, I said, "I am going to marry her!" Seven months later we walked down the aisle together. Beth would say, "Did you really think that?" "Of Course, you are the inspiration of my life, my poetry." Do you remember that a few days after you smiled at me, I wrote you this note:

> How do I love you?
> Let me count the ways.

A. Allow. Allow the person with Alzheimer's to talk without correcting them. If what they want to do is not hurting themselves or others,
let them do it.

T. Tenderness. We practice tenderness with children. Persons suffering from Alzheimer's often revert to childhood ways. They are still adults, and they need to be treated with dignity as adults. I remember counseling one family where the wife who had Alzheimer's would run and hide in the closet if someone rang the doorbell. I discovered that she was abused as a child.

Fortunately, my wife has not displayed dementia symptoms. She was lovingly nurtured as a child. After I prepare her meal, she will say, "Thank you, for fixing this good meal." Tenderness is reciprocal.

I. Imagination. Try to imagine how you would feel if you were the Alzheimer's patient. Through the years I heard Alzheimer's patients say, "I don't want to be a burden on anyone." When Beth says that now, I say, "You are not a burden, this is payback time. You did these things for me for 55 years. Now I can do more for you, and that gives me joy."

O. Offer. Offer to help when needed but let them do things for themselves whenever possible.
I am responsible for preparing all our meals now. When I start, Beth will almost always say,
how can I help? It would be easier for me to say, "That is ok, I will do everything." However, I usually say, "You can come sit at the counter, and help."
I will give her the butter, slices of bread; and say, "you can butter some bread to toast."

N. Nurture. Nature is nurturing and healing. Harvard professor, E. O. Wilson, biologists, ecologist, entomologist, and naturalist, said prior to his death in 2021, that we need to speak in a clear voice, using science and the humanities, to bring the hope of healing for our hurting world. As a naturalist, Wilson spent a lot of time in the beauty of nature. This shaped his vision of healing. God so loved the world
—Love incarnated in tender teachings. Healing brokenness, saving all. When nature speaks our soul is revitalized.

Orpheus charmed animals with his music. His singing made the trees shiver.
Orpheus even charmed the stones.

The Orpheus voice speaks by listening.
He sees with words coming from inside space. His seeing invited all creation to join in concertos.

The beauty and wonder of nature has healing powers that link possibility with actuality. Contemplating the beauty of birds and flowers warms our heart with healing love energies, nurtures the soul.

This soul nurturing in beauty and goodness leads to kindness in family living.

A. Allow. Allow times each day to contemplate on what you desire for your family and yourself:
- To be safe and secure
- To be happy and at peace
- To have good health
- To be free from fear
- To have fun times for all in family

To see beauty in all people, animals, and all living things

L. Love. Love is everything. In the Bible, love is everything.
The heartbeat of Jesus' teaching is what we know as the Great Commandment. When someone asked Jesus what the greatest commandment in the Law was, Jesus replied: "**Love the Lord your God with all your**

heart and with all your soul and with all your mind. This is the first and greatest commandment. And the second is like it: Love your neighbor as yourself."

Conclusion

Alzheimer's

Expressed in a haiku and a sonnet, this is my personal pain—

I touch the pain
of Alzheimer's each day
It doesn't go away

Life After Alzheimer's

Alzheimer's, a thief I did not invite!
Came through locked doors to steal
memory after memory from my wife.
Now she does not remember what is real.

I remember the joys of former days.
Dancing in sunshine, dancing in rain.
Must I learn to love in new ways?
Take her hand and dance with pain.

Memories of blue bird skies dripping—
Dripping down my cheeks and chin.
Will life ever be whole and sane again?

Must I learn to dance in new rhythm?
Hold pain close to beating heart.
Alzheimer's, a thief I did not invite!

Appendix: Key Biblical Verses
That Support Relational Kindness

1. God's love and **kindness** will shine upon us like the sun that rises in the sky. On us who live in the dark shadow of death, this light will shine to guide us into a life of peace" (Luke 1:78-79).

2. Jesus said, "Come to me, all of you who are tired from carrying heavy loads, and I will give your rest. Take my yoke and put it on you, and learn from me, because I am **gentle and humble in spirit**; and you will find rest. For the yoke I will give you is easy and the load I will put on you is light." (Matthew 11:28-30).

3. Jesus said, "**Blessed are the gentle**, they will receive what God has promised!" (Matthew 5:5).

4. Jesus taught, "People who are well do not need a doctor, but only those who are sick. Go and find out what is meant by the scripture that says, 'It is **kindness** that I want, not animal sacrifices.' I have not come to call respectable people, but outcasts." (Matthew 9:12-13)

5. "A man with leprosy came to Jesus and knelt down. **Jesus felt sorry for him,** so he put his hands on him and said, 'You are well.'" (Mark 1:40-41).

6. "Jesus said, "Don't worry about your life. **God will take care of you**." (Luke 12:22-26).

7. Paul in imitating the spirit of Jesus, grounds kindness in the being of God, "You are God's people so **be gentle, kind, humble, and meek**." (Colossians 3:12).

8. "**Be kind and merciful**, and forgive others, just as God forgave you because of Jesus." (Ephesians 4:32).

9. "I pray that you will **be blessed with kindness** and peace from God, who is and was and is coming. May you receive kindness and peace from Jesus, the faithful witness." (Revelation 1:4-5).

10. "I pray that **Jesus will be kind to all of you**." (Revelation 22:21).

BOOKS BY DWAYNE COLE

A Center that Holds: Adventures in Kindness

Alpenglow Miracles: Fire Dance of Wonder.

Alzheimer's: A Minister's Guide

A Prayer of Blessing: As You Go Remember This

A Relational Hermeneutic of Kindness

A Relational Trinity of Kindness

BEARS AND MOOSE OF ALASKA: Nature Poetry

Black-Capped Chickadees: Messengers of Good News Clouds of Inspiration

Down on the Farm in Georgia: A Poetic Memoir

Dragonfly Magic

Gentle Galilean Glories: The Tender Teachings of Jesus

God and Evil: An Ode to Kindness

Heart Haiku: Alaska Inspired Photo and Poems

Heart Sijo: Alaska Inspired Photo and Poems

Jesus' Transforming Beatitudes: Selected Sermons from Year A

Jesus' Transforming Love: Selected Sermons from Year B

Jesus' Transforming Gentle Teachings: Selected Sermons from Year C

Kindness Is Every Step

Lone Leaf Dancing

Poems Inspired by Process Philosophy

Poet of the Universe: A Vision of Beauty and Goodness.

Rainbows of Hope

Snowshoe Hare Beauty

Steller's Jay Blue Sway

The Apostles' Creed: A Living Creed for the Living Church.

The Bible: A Poetic Journey

The Book of Revelation: Jesus' Kindness Transforms Suffering

The Serenity Prayer: A Pathway to Peace and Happiness

The Story of the Bible: Authority, Inspiration, Canonization, Translation

TREES AND DRIFTWOOD: Poetic Ecology

When Flowers Speak, Listen

When Stones Speak

WINGS OF INSPIRATION

Write down your personal questions and thoughts about Alzheimer's on the following blank pages. Send them to me: *tadpolejr@aol,com* and share them with your Primary Care Physician.

www.ingramcontent.com/pod-product-compliance
Lightning Source LLC
Chambersburg PA
CBHW061806070526
44586CB00023B/2737